MW01599707

Presented to

my Daddy god

On

Sheila

By

_____

My Son, Verses from the Book of Proverbs
ISBN: 978-0-9847887-1-2
Copyright © 2012. Viji Roberts. All Rights Reserved.
Photography: Praveen Thekkat

Scripture taken from the New King James Version.
Copyright © 1982 by Thomas Nelson, Inc. Used by permission.
All Rights Reserved.

Printed in the United States of America
First Printing 2012

Davidson Publishing
www.davidsonpublishing.org

Introduction

This book contains most of the 'My Son' passages from the Book of Proverbs arranged as life lessons from A to Z.

Inspired by the Spirit of God, King Solomon committed to pass on what he learned to the next generation. So growing up, my mother highlighted in my Bible these verses; and while the idea was to return me to the Bible, her intent and the message left a deep impact. Words of wisdom indeed!

I have learned life lessons from these verses; verses I have found to be a dependable foundation for all my decisions and living. I hope to return the favor by passing on the legacy of learning and wisdom as my son turns 18.

Whatever the relationship, teacher-student; mentor-mentee; elder-disciple; parent-child, these lessons are applicable. Neither are they limited to 'sons.' You can even gift yourself with these timeless lessons.

Even as men and women have found solace, guidance, and wisdom through centuries, I pray that generations of men and women would benefit from the words of Solomon, the wisest man who ever lived. More importantly, that they would learn from the heart of our Lord Jesus Christ to whom be honor and glory forever and ever.

Amen

3-Step process of application

Read it quick.
Read it slow.
Read it till you get the flow.

May God make you wiser as you apply these principles!

Turn and look under each stone
what treasures God has hid.
Each verse, each word to feast on,
His children, He does bid.

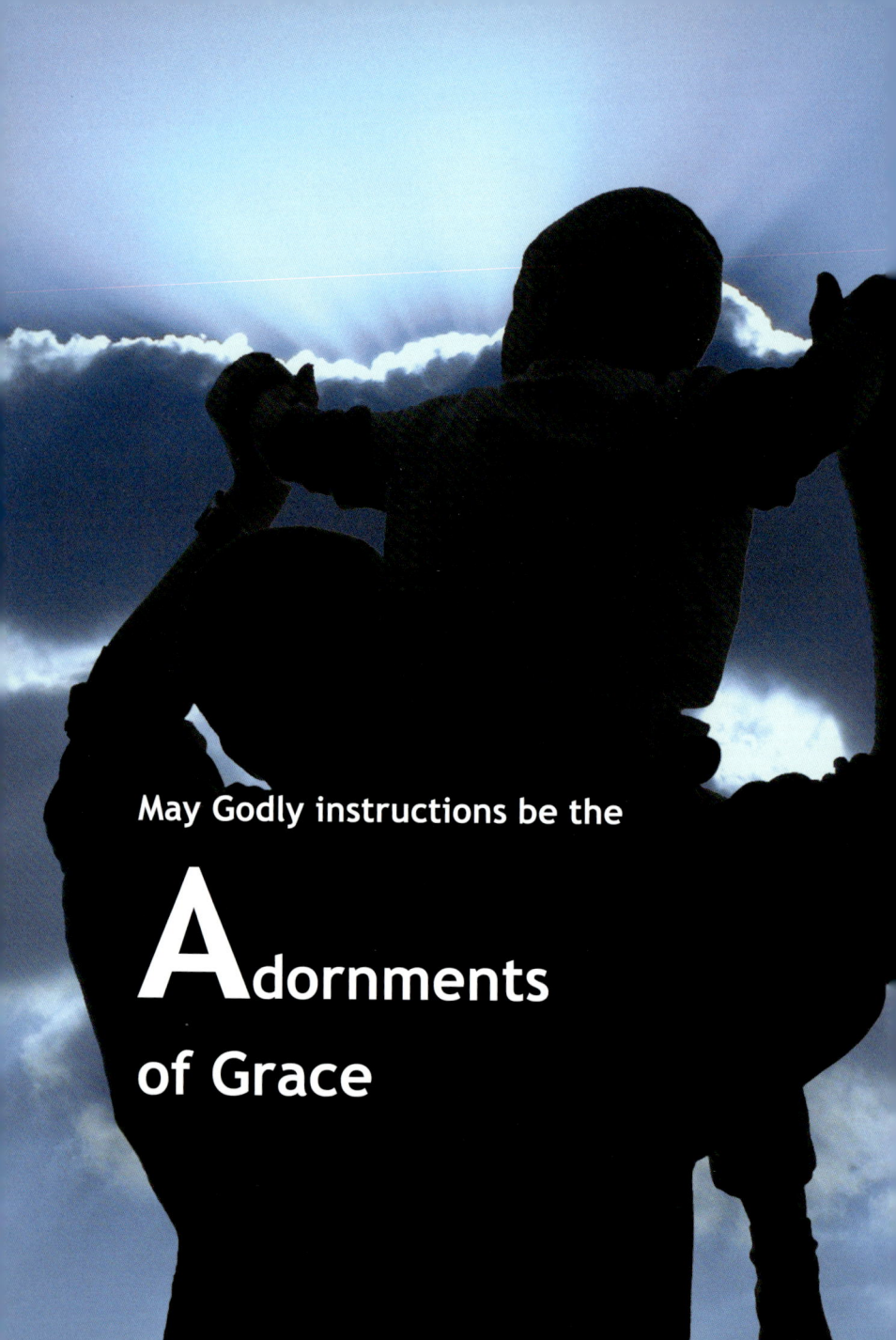

May Godly instructions be the

Adornments

of Grace

Adornment

(n) something that adds attractiveness.

My son,
hear the instruction of your father,
And do not forsake the law of your mother;
For they will be a graceful ornament on your head,
And chains about your neck.

Proverbs 1: 8-9

Bind

these lessons close, so as to have them available all times.

Bind

(v) to fasten or secure.

My son,

keep your father's command,

And do not forsake the law of your mother.

Bind them continually upon your heart,

tie them around your neck.

When you roam, they will lead you;

When you sleep, they will keep you;

And when you awake, they will speak with you.

For the commandment is a lamp,

And the law a light;

Reproofs of instruction are the way of life,

To keep you from the evil woman,

From the flattering tongue of a seductress..

Proverbs 6: 20-24

Correction is the vehicle that
carries God's concern and care.

It is a joy to see what God is making of you.

Correct

(v) to make or set right.

My son,
do not despise
the chastening of the LORD,
Nor detest His correction;
For whom the LORD loves He corrects,
Just as a father the son in whom
he delights.

Proverbs 3:11-12

Be cautious to

Discern Good and Evil.

Ungodly opportunities sometimes come wrapped in good purpose and great prospect.

Discern

(v) to see or understand the difference.

My son, if sinners entice you,
Do not consent.
If they say, "Come with us,
Let us lie in wait to shed blood;
Let us lurk secretly for the innocent without cause;
Let us swallow them alive like Sheol,
And whole, like those who go down to the Pit;
We shall find all kinds of precious possessions,
We shall fill our houses with spoil;
Cast in your lot among us,
Let us all have one purse"
My son, do not walk in the way with them,
Keep your foot from their path;

Proverbs 1:10-15

Focus your **E**yes
on wisdom and discretion.
A full life and strength of character
belong to those who are godly focused.

Eyes

(n) something central.

My son,

let them not depart from your eyes

--Keep sound wisdom and discretion;

So they will be life to your soul

And grace to your neck.

Proverbs 3:21-22

17

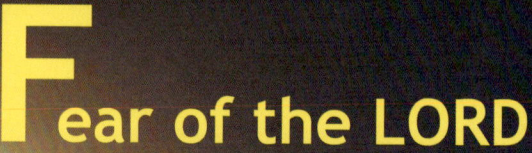

Fear of the LORD

is true worship.
Stick by it; for the world
will try its best to
wean you off
godly reverence.

Fear

(v) to have a reverential awe.

My son,
fear the LORD and the king;
Do not associate with those
given to change;

Proverbs 24:21

"The Lord bless you and keep you;
The Lord make His face shine upon you,
And be gracious to you;
The Lord lift up His countenance upon you,
And give you peace."

We pray and promise that neither sands
of time nor trial would make us

Give Up

on you.

Give Up

(v) to cease doing or attempting something.

Chasten your son
while there is hope,
And do not set
your heart
on his destruction.

Proverbs 19:18

Heed

and understand
wisdom so that you may
be the epitome of
wisdom and knowledge.

Heed

(v) to pay attention.

My son,
pay attention to my wisdom;
Lend your ear to my understanding,
That you may preserve discretion,
And your lips may keep knowledge.

Proverbs 5:1-2

To be effective, it is **I**mportant to be loving, timely and fair.

Godly corrections demonstrate both love for God and for you.

Important

(adj.) valuable in content or relationship.

He who spares his rod hates his son,
But he who loves him
disciplines him promptly.

Proverbs 13:24

Learn to **J**udge things not people.

Learn to differentiate wisdom from the noise of its raw delivery.

Judge

(v) to form an
estimate or
evaluation of.

Cease listening to instruction,
my son,
And you will stray from the words
of knowledge.

Proverbs 19:27

Keep

the Law of the LORD.

Not in the letter of the law,
but in love
for God.

For him the
LORD hears.

Keep

(v) to conform to in habits or conduct.

Whoever keeps
the law is a discerning son,
But a companion of gluttons
shames his father.
One who increases his possessions
by usury and extortion
Gathers it for him who will pity the poor.
One who turns away his ear
from hearing the law,
Even his prayer is an
abomination.

Proverbs 28: 7-9

29

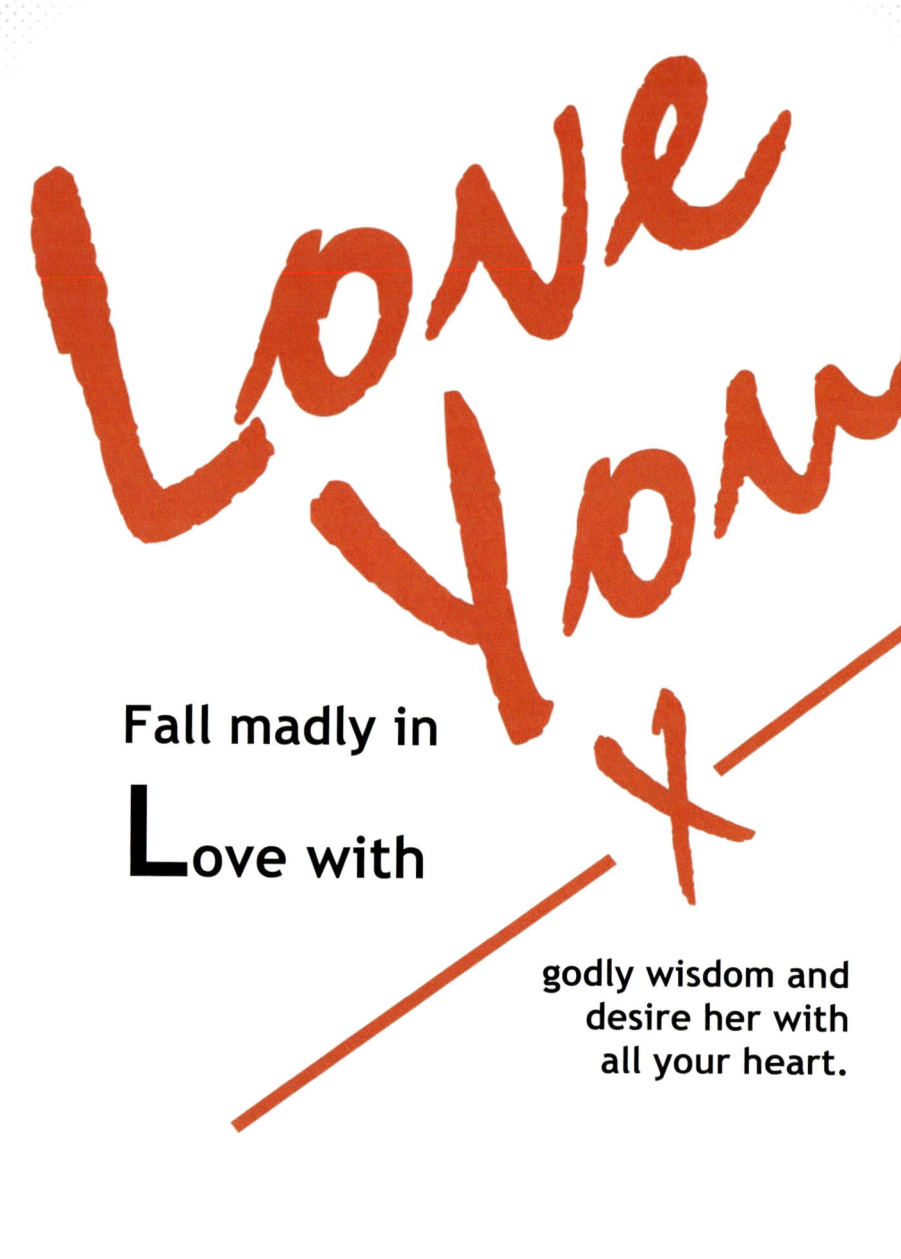

Love You x

Fall madly in **L**ove with

godly wisdom and desire her with all your heart.

Love

(v) to hold dear: cherish.

Get wisdom! Get understanding!
Do not forget, nor turn away from the words of my
mouth.
Do not forsake her, and she will preserve you;
Love her, and she will keep you.
Wisdom is the principal thing;
Therefore get wisdom.

And in all your getting, get understanding.
Exalt her, and she will promote you;
She will bring you honor, when you embrace her.
She will place on your head an ornament of grace;
A crown of glory she will deliver to you."

Proverbs 4:5-9

Mind
your step.
Each step, each day.

Put your heart
to everything you do;
and do it as unto the
Lord.

Mind

(v) to pay attention.

Hear, my son,
and be wise;
And guide your heart in
the way.

Proverbs 23:19

Don't **N**eglect to listen just because it sounds like nagging. Be inclined to act on them.

Neglect

(v) to leave undone
through carelessness.

My son,
give attention to my words;
Incline your ear to
my sayings.

Proverbs 4:20

Don't miss out
on God given

Opportunities.

...they
sometimes
come packaged
in time capsules
with short expirations.

Opportunity

(n) a good chance
for advancement
or progress.

He who gathers
in summer is a wise son;
He who sleeps in harvest is
a son who causes shame.

Proverbs 10:5

Application of information
will pave your way to

godly **P**rosperity
and a good life.

Prosperity

(n) the condition
of being successful
or thriving.

Hear, my son,
and receive my sayings,
And the years of your life
will be many.

Proverbs 4:10

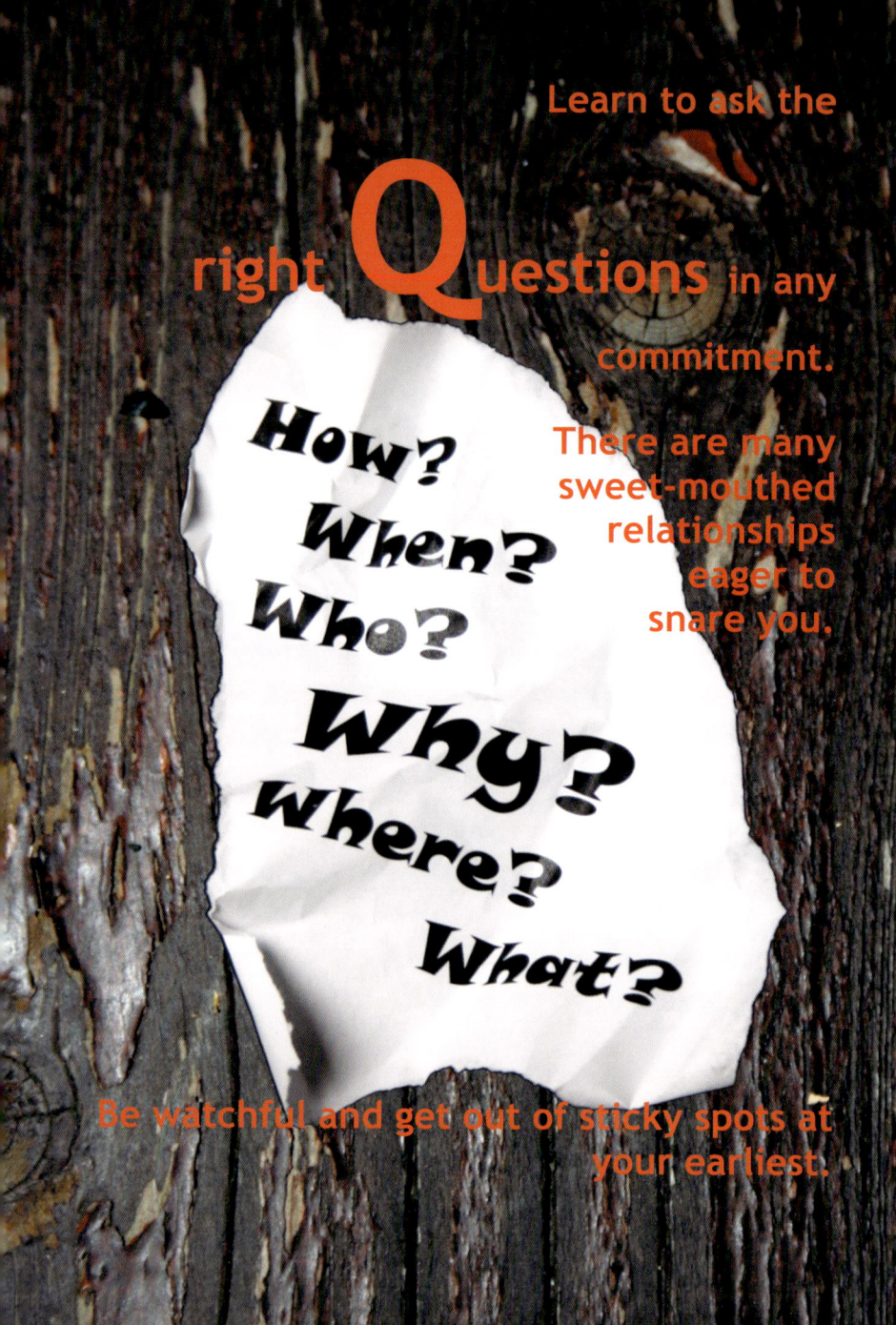

Question

(n) an act or instance of asking.

My son,
if you become surety for your friend,
If you have shaken hands in pledge for a stranger,
You are snared by the words of your mouth;
You are taken by the words of your mouth.
So do this, my son, and deliver yourself;
For you have come into the hand of your friend:
Go and humble yourself;
Plead with your friend.
Give no sleep to your eyes,
Nor slumber to your eyelids.
Deliver yourself like a gazelle from the hand [of the hunter],
And like a bird from the hand of the fowler.

Proverbs 6:1-3

Rebuke

is hard, even
when lovingly intended.

Our prayer is that it may fall
softly on your soul
and bear a good fruit.

Rebuke
(v) to turn back.

A wise son heeds
his father's instruction,
But a scoffer
does not listen to rebuke.

Proverbs 13:1

Watch out for worldly

Sensuality.

Keep yourself for the woman God has prepared for you.

Sensuality

(n) excessive pursuit in the gratification of the senses.

For why should you, my son,
be enraptured by
an immoral woman,
And be embraced
in the arms of a seductress?

Proverbs 5:20

Treasure

words of experience.
Make them your closest
possessions
and your most
valuable assets.

Treasure

(n) esteemed as
rare or precious.

My son, keep my words,
And treasure my commands within you.
Keep my commands and live,
And my law as the apple of your eye.
Bind them on your fingers;
Write them on the tablet of your heart.
Say to wisdom, "You are my sister,"
And call understanding your nearest kin,

Proverbs 7:1-4

Be passionate about

Understanding

the Fear of the Lord and
finding the Knowledge of God.

You will find that these
are more than
mere silver linings
in your life's
journey.

Understand

(v) to grasp the meaning of.

My son, if you receive my words,
And treasure my commands within you,
So that you incline your ear to wisdom,
And apply your heart to understanding;
Yes, if you cry out for discernment,
And lift up your voice for understanding,
If you seek her as silver,
And search for her as for hidden treasures;
Then you will understand the fear of the LORD,
And find the knowledge of God.

Proverbs 2:1-5

Foolish Vs. Wise

the choice is clear.

The joy over your success is not for ourselves, but for you.

May you be a winner in the Lord.

AND THE WINNER IS...

Versus

(prep.) in contrast
to or as the
alternative of.

A wise son
makes a father glad,
But a foolish man despises
his mother.

Proverbs 15:20

A **W**ise Heart

brings joy to all those it meets.

Wise

(adj.) exercising or showing sound judgment.

My son,
if your heart is wise,
My heart will rejoice--indeed,
I myself;

Proverbs 23:15

Pursue what is

X' cellent.

Make that your life's creed.

X'cellent

(adj.) eminently good.

My son, eat honey because it is good,

And the honeycomb which is sweet to your taste;

So shall the knowledge of wisdom be to your soul;

If you have found it, there is a prospect,

And your hope will not be cut off.

Proverbs 24:13-14

The secret of living a godly life
is not trusting

Your own heart

but God's.

Acknowledge Him as Lord
in all your ways,
and He will show you the
right way.

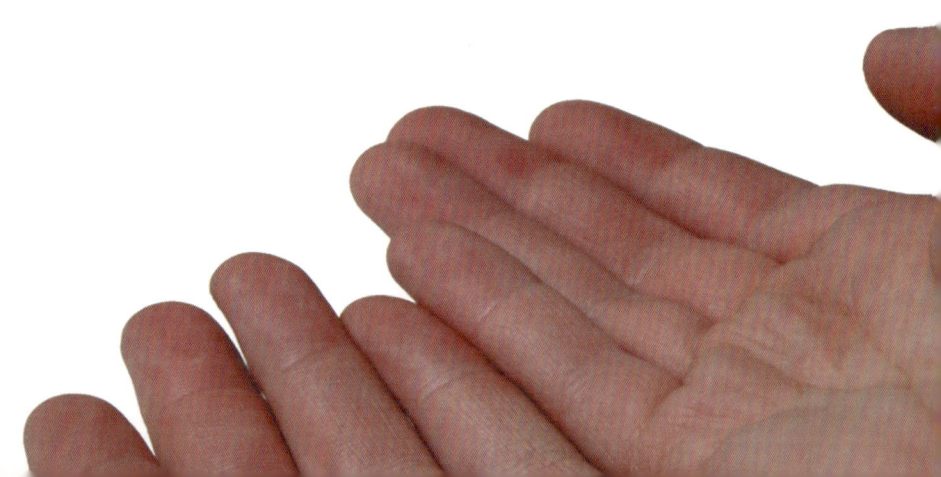

Your

(adj.) relating to oneself.

My son, do not forget my law,
But let your heart keep my commands;
For length of days and long life
And peace they will add to you.
Let not mercy and truth forsake you;
Bind them around your neck,
Write them on the tablet of your heart,
And so find favor and high esteem
In the sight of God and man.
Trust in the Lord with all your heart,
And lean not on your own understanding;
In all your ways acknowledge Him,
And He shall direct your paths.
Do not be wise in your own eyes;
Fear the Lord and depart from evil.

Proverbs 3:1-7

Z

is not the end;
it is the beginning
of application.

Instructions end
when learning occurs

Z

(n.) last letter of the English alphabet.

What, my son?
And what, son of my womb?
And what, son of my vows?
Do not give your strength to women,
Nor your ways to that which destroys kings.

Open your mouth for the speechless,
In the cause of all who are appointed to die.
Open your mouth, judge righteously,
And plead the cause of the poor and needy.

Proverbs 31: 1-3, 8-9

Life is about making choices!

My son, you will find
that life brings with it many choices.

When in such a bind
to discern from its many voices.

Make up your mind
and choose in spite the noises;

To discern the godly kind
in which God's heart rejoices.

Acknowledgements

I want to thank my Lord Jesus Christ for the privilege of laboring for Him. As I was thinking on what I could give my son as he turns eighteen, the idea for this book was planted in my mind.

The transition from the idea to the book you hold in your hand is because of family and friends. I thank my godly parents for bringing me up in the fear of the Lord and for their continued encouragement. Thanks to Joyce, my wife of twenty years, and my wonderful sisters-in-law, Biji, Sajini and Bincy, who made me feel like a million bucks as I shared the idea with them. Also, a special shout-out to Priscilla, my cousin, from the west coast.

Special thanks for the valuable feedback and encouragement of my friends Dwight Knight, K V Simon, and Susan Renu Philips. Heartfelt thanks to Kris Ryckman and his son, Kayden for their willingness to come out for the photographs. Thanks to Praveen, and especially his wife, Malathy, who was willing to spare Praveen for the long hours this project required.

Thanks to Paul Varghese and Davidson Publishing, for believing in the project and standing behind this both in prayer and by providing all the necessary support.

About the Author

Viji and Joyce Roberts live in Mississauga, Ontario with their son Daniel. They are involved actively in their local church, where Viji serves as an Elder. Viji is a Corporate Trainer and loves to design and deliver training that makes a difference.

His heart for missions and the next generation is evident as he sits on the board of MSC Canada and is actively involved in many committees, both in the Church and in the community.

Joyce works with a local company dividing time between work, home and mentoring young women.

Daniel is preparing to pursue a career in business.

Life Lessons

Life Lessons

Life Lessons

Life Lessons

Life Lessons

Life Lessons